How to read Bible references:

Matthew 24:35 = The Gospel according to Matthew, chapter 24, verse 35

Word of Hope Ministries

ISBN: 978-1-908392-05-3

Love my enemies! Is it possible?

E.M. Hicham

Serious Answers to Sincere Questions

remain for a short while before returning to Nazareth where He was brought up. When He was about 30 years old He had gone to the river Jordan where He was baptised by His cousin, John the Baptist. That was the beginning of His public ministry. He had begun to go about doing good: saving, teaching, healing and transforming lives. The common people heard Him gladly. Wherever He went great crowds would come to witness His miracles, to seek His help, but particularly, to listen to His teaching. His popularity incensed the religious rulers of the Jews, who had become increasingly envious, and at last their jealousy drove them to engage in a plot to do away with Jesus of Nazareth once and for all.

And so Jesus was carried away to the place of crucifixion. There He was nailed to the cross which was on the ground. Then the cross would be lifted up. It would be carried to its socket and dropped into that socket. At that moment all the bones of our Lord (in fulfilment of King David's prophecy in Psalm 22) would have become dislocated. There in agony and burning pain Jesus was crucified; He was on the middle cross, with a criminal being crucified on either side of Him.

As the crucifixion took place the nails were hammered into His wrists and feet. Instead of swearing and blaspheming, Jesus prayed tenderly for His executioners! From that central cross, Jesus began to speak. The first thing He said was, "Father forgive them, for they do not know what they do." (Bible, Luke 23: 34)

A remarkable prayer!

It is not wrong, says the Bible, for Christians to pray for themselves. Sometimes when we are in great trouble we do pray for ourselves. Frequently in the Bible we find men and women of God praying for themselves; especially when they are surrounded with troubles or enemies. Often in the Bible we find people praying for others; but they are usually their friends. But when Jesus was overwhelmed with pain and surrounded by persecutors; when He was going through the greatest trouble the world has witnessed, we do not find Him praying for Himself, but for others. The others for whom He prayed are the very enemies who have done such spiteful acts to Him.

It's a unique prayer!

In the original, the sense of what Jesus did was that it was continuous.

Jesus not only prayed, but kept on praying. It means that Jesus did not only pray once, but as they hurt Him He prayed repeatedly the same prayer. So we can image that as they drove the nails into His wrists and feet, He was praying, "Father forgive them." As they lifted up the cross and it shuddered as it fell into its socket (and there was this unspeakable agony which would make all normal people scream), at that stage too there came from the lips of Jesus this same prayer, "Father forgive them". As the people began to go by, especially the religious leaders and the authorities who said, "He saved others; let Him save Himself if He is the Christ, the chosen of God", and as they sneered at the shame and the pain of Jesus, nothing came from his lips except, "Father forgive them for they do not know what they do". Also at the foot of the cross there were soldiers who were so hardened to crucifixion and the sufferings of others that they gambled away His clothes. Yet over their heads comes the voice of the suffering Saviour Jesus praying the same prayer, "Father forgive them".

We think about the nobility of the Son of God. It's not many days since those hands were stretched out to heal, to comfort and to bless. Those same hands took up children! It's not many days ago that those feet which were cruelly pierced, walked to houses of sorrow. It's not long ago that that side which soon was going to be pierced with a spear was the side into which the young children nestled. Jesus Christ could no longer move to touch and to help, but He could and did pray, "Father forgive them."

Not just a man of words!

It was at the very moment when people were doing their worst that Jesus said, "Father forgive them"! He prayed for their forgiveness. He prayed for forgiveness for the murderous, bigoted religious leaders. He prayed forgiveness for the howling mob. He prayed forgiveness for the soldiers. As someone put it, He threw a mountain of prayer around them all. And we are reminded again that just three years before, on a different hill, He had said, "Love your enemies, do good to those who hate you, bless those who curse you, and pray for those who spitefully use you" (Bible, Luke 6:27,28). And here at His crucifixion He was practising His own teaching because Jesus wasn't just a man of words; He practised what He preached to others. He wasn't a hypocrite. He was praying that the greatest need of the people around Him would be met (your greatest need is the same!) - that they will have their sins forgiven.

What did Jesus pray for?

Now the word 'forgive' here is a wonderful word in the New Testament. It is sometimes translated forgive and sometimes translated suffer. For example, one day people brought infants to Jesus that He might touch them; but when the disciples saw it, they rebuked them. But Jesus called them to Him and said, "Suffer the little children to come unto Me." (Bible, Luke 18:16) In other words, Jesus was saying, "Let the little children come to me, and do not hinder them." That is the same word he uses when He prayed, "Father forgive them." What He meant when He spoke about the children was this: "Do not interfere with the children. Don't stop them coming to Me. Don't step in to the situation." When you understand that, you understand what Jesus was really praying on the cross.

He was basically praying, "Father, don't interfere with what they are doing, for they are doing it in ignorance. Don't step in to the situation and damn them. Don't come into the situation and judge them. Don't do it now Father. Postpone Your judgment so that they will have the opportunity to understand the awfulness of what they are doing, to repent and to receive forgiveness." There were legions of angels ready as Jesus Christ was on the cross, ready to deliver Him. God could have stepped in with an almighty act, struck all His opponents dead and removed them forever; but Jesus prayed that His Father would postpone the judgment.

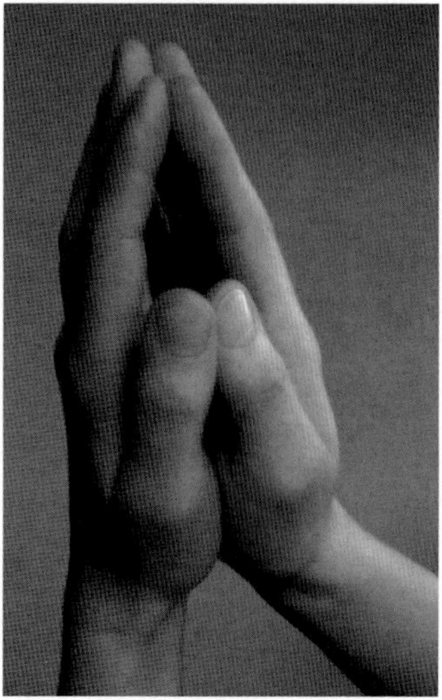

The whole message of the cross radiates forgiveness. The whole cross is about forgiveness. I am very glad that when I first heard of Jesus Christ and His message God didn't step in straight away and judge me for my awful attitude to Christ. I hated Christians and the Bible. I despised the Jesus Christ of the Bible and His message for months and years. I continued with my sins not realising the enormity of them. If God had stepped in then and had judged me then or removed me from this life then, I would have been damned everlastingly and deservedly so. But God restrained His judgment. I believe He did this in response to the intercession of Christ on the cross. God restrained His judgment and I was permitted at last to hear the gospel, the good news of Jesus (which you are hearing now!) and to enter into the experience of forgiveness. The place where I found forgiveness was at Calvary where Jesus had first prayed, "Father forgive for they do not know what they do"!

Hatred was everywhere! But Jesus chose to love.

What does Jesus' prayer teach us?

When we look at what people did to Jesus, we often try to detach ourselves from the scene. We say, 'We were not part of it'. We think how awful those people were and feel that we would not want anything to do with people like that. We would not want to have had any part in the crucifixion of Jesus.

We need to remember that the very sins which are seen at Calvary have parallels in our own hearts. Why did Judas betray Christ? Well, he was the man who kept the money bag. He kept the common treasury of the twelve disciples. We read in the Bible (John's gospel) that he "was a thief, and had the money box; and he used to take what was put in it" (Bible, John 12:5-6). But he wanted a little bit more. So he was willing to give information about the whereabouts of Christ so that it would be easy to arrest Him without a public riot. He sold the information for thirty pieces of silver. One sin which put Christ on the cross is that one man wanted a little bit more for himself! It is sin like that that crucified Christ.

Then there were the chief priests (the religious leaders) who were willing to pay the thirty pieces of silver because they were jealous. They were jealous that Jesus Christ was popular and they were not; that the whole city went out to meet Him and they were just left behind. They were burning with jealousy. He was good and just and holy. There was no fault in Him. Yet although there was no fault in Him their hearts were filled with murderous thoughts towards Him. And those murderous thoughts were stocked up in their hearts by nothing else except envy.

Do we not have the same problem in our lives? Often we look at another person who is good or no worse than ourselves, we look at someone who is in a public position or getting some attention, then we are jealous without any rational explanation. It is a sin which shows the depravity of our hearts. It was jealousy that crucified Jesus Christ. Without greed and jealousy, Jesus would never have gone to the cross!

And then there was Pilate the governor. He gave in. He had made up his mind not to crucify Christ, but the people prevailed against him. They put pressure on him. He knew that if he didn't give in, his own prestige would suffer. He had a certain image which he wanted to maintain. He wanted to leave a certain impression in people's minds. In the end he was willing to stand down on any principle as long as his prestige would remain intact. If that meant the death of someone who was innocent, so be it. But whatever happened, his own image must remain intact.

Friend, the sins which put Christ on the cross are sins that feature in our lives too: wanting a little bit more, jealousy and self-love. We cannot detach ourselves from Calvary. We too have our part in the crucifixion of the Son of God. Although we were not there physically, it was our sins that nailed Him to the cross as He took the punishment in our place.

So, loving my enemies, is it possible?

Paul - a terrorist who became a preacher of the Gospel.[1]

Saul of Tarsus was the chief persecutor of early Christians. A very zealous Jew, He was an enemy to the Christian Church. He was a murderer. He put (and probably killed) innocent Christian people in prison and delighted in doing it. He hated Jesus Christ and His name

[1]There is a DVD called Damascus produced by Syrian actors which portrays the life of Paul. Contact us for more details.

and His people and His work and His word. But he had a dramatic encounter with the risen Christ. As Saul was on his way to Damascus, filled with threats and fury, he was stopped in his tracks by Jesus Christ Himself who said, "Saul, Saul, why are you persecuting Me?" (Bible, Acts 9:4) It was Jesus' call which changed him. He was transformed from Saul, the enemy of Christianity, to Paul, the main propagator of its message. He left his position of prestige in Jewish society, to become a travelling missionary who experienced incredible suffering in order to share the message of Christ throughout the Roman empire. Later he wrote a letter to a church saying, 'I have been crucified with Christ. It is no longer I who live, but Christ lives in me; the life which I now live in the flesh I live by faith in the Son of God (Jesus)[2], who loved me and gave Himself for me' (Bible, Galatians 2:20). That was the secret of Paul's love for his 'enemies.' You cannot love your enemies in your own strength, but Christ will give you the ability to love as you trust Him and obey His commands. The Bible says, 'I can do all things through Christ who strengthens me.' (Bible, Philippians 4.13)

Joon Gon Kim - a Korean who loved his enemies

Many other men and women in recent decades have dedicated their lives to spreading the Christian message, often braving torture and death. For example, in Korea, Joon Gon Kim, a well-known Christian leader, witnessed his wife and father slaughtered before his eyes by

[2]E.M. Hicham has written a booklet called, 'How can God have a Son?' Contact us if you would like a free copy.

Communist sympathizers from his own village. He himself was beaten senseless and left for dead. He survived the beating and asked God to give him love for the souls of his enemies. He was eventually instrumental in the conversion of 30 Communists to Christ, including the person responsible for the death of his family members!

Kamal - A radical Egyptian terrorist changed from a murderous person to a forgiving person

Kamal started memorizing the Qur'an at a very early age and developed what he called 'a love for the word of God'. As he grew older, he started reading books on Islam and the interpretation of the Qur'an. By sorting out Muslims from non-Muslims according to the Qur'an's teaching, he ended up considering his own parents infidels. Little things such as a woman not wearing a veil would make her a non-Muslim according to the way he understood the Qur'an. If a man didn't grow a beard he would be considered a non-Muslim. He considered Christians as his worst enemies and started getting involved in attacks against Christians and churches. An Islamic Group, dedicated to the overthrow of the secular government of Egypt and the installation of a strict Muslim government, recruited him into their ranks, appointing him as a local leader. His group became involved in kidnapping a famous moderate Muslim writer who had dared to criticize the Islamic Group.

Upon reading an article in the Cairo newspaper about Christians arrested in Egypt for proselytizing, Kamal and his group decided that

it was "past time" to do something for the sake of Islam. Given their small numbers, however, they decided their battle would be an intellectual one, researching and writing a book proving that Mohammed is the true prophet of God, and that the Bible of the Christians and Jews is a corrupted text. Kamal was chosen by his Emir (leader), the leader of the Islamic Group, to do the research and write the book. He objected strenuously at first, but eventually took on the job, which he described as the "most distasteful thing" he had ever done.

When he had completed reading the Bible and cross-referencing what he had read with numerous Islamic books, Kamal was astonished to discover that the Bible was neither inaccurate nor corrupted. Instead, he was astonished at the Bible's teachings on forgiveness and unconditional love, as reflected in the life and words of Jesus. He was particularly stunned to read how Jesus had warned his followers about persecution and how, two thousand years later, that persecution was taking place exactly as Jesus had said it would. His reading of the Bible helped him understand why Christians in Egypt never retaliated against Muslims, and why they were able to forgive and forget. As much as he hated reading the Bible, he fell in love with its message and teachings.

Nonetheless, he had a job to do, and he continued with dogged determination, electing to prove that Jesus is not God and was never crucified. Studying the Qur'an for this purpose, he put together all of

God's qualities and attributes as the Qur'an talks about them, and then searched the Qur'an for Jesus' attributes. To his dismay, Kamal discovered that many attributes the Qur'an assigned to God are also assigned to Jesus, proving to Kamal that Jesus and God are, indeed, one.

Growing doubts now made Kamal's life miserable. He had always loved Islam and believed that the only way to God was through Mohammed. But if Jesus and God are one, then what is the way to heaven?

One day, the Emir came to visit Kamal in his house and discovered all the research that Kamal had documented (the deity of Jesus, the Bible being the true Word of God, etc.). He couldn't believe what he read. He told Kamal that he would kill him if he shared his heretical ideas with any Muslim and that he was now considered an infidel.

Kamal, however, could not turn from the conviction that Christianity was the right way. He sat down and said, "God you know that I love you, and I know that you want me on the right path. God, I can't resist anymore. All that I did, I did trying to please you. Please help me."

Jesus heard his prayer. He saved him. He gave him a new heart and new life. Kamal's search for reconciliation started with his mother. He begged her forgiveness for his years of harshness and ill treatment of the family. His search for reconciliation didn't end with his family either. He sought out the Christian owners of businesses whom he had robbed, or mistreated, and begged their forgiveness too.

Over the ensuing months, Kamal grew in his new faith, gradually winning the confidence and trust of local Christians and finding fellowship at a church. He was baptized and continues to brave physical attacks and threats against his life, because he feels that no price is too great to pay for the One who gave everything for him, Jesus.[3]

Conclusion

Loving your enemy is not just a matter of thinking nice thoughts. By your own efforts you can never succeed. "With men it is impossible, but not with God; for with God all things are possible." (Bible, Mark 10: 27). You need Jesus to change your heart because the heart of our problems is the problem of our hearts. You need Jesus to give you the kind of love that God showed when He sent Jesus to save and forgive a world full of despicable people; God-hating, vulgar, foul-mouthed, unfaithful, lying, cheating, stealing, selfish people. The list goes on, describing us at our worst. Yet God loved us. We can only love like that if Jesus Christ is working in our lives. When we trust Christ, God, by His Holy Spirit, comes to dwell in our hearts. "If anyone is in Christ, he is a new creation; old things have passed away; behold, all things have become new." (Bible, 2Corinthians 5:17)

Jesus lived the perfect life that we should have lived, and He died the death that we deserve to die. He died to bear the punishment for

[3]*The story of Kamal is used with the kind permission of the More Than Dreams Ministry.*

our wrongdoing. His death satisfied the justice and love of God. By trusting in what Jesus has done for us, we can know that our sins are forgiven. Our relationship with our Creator will be restored. God will give us a new heart, a forgiven heart and help us to live increasingly, to love and serve Him!

If you would like to receive further information, please contact us.

If you wish to make further study of the Christian faith, correspondence courses in English, Arabic and French are available from:

Word of Hope Ministries
22 New Street,
Rochdale,
OL16 3PQ,
United Kingdom

Email: **word.hope@gmail.com**
Web: **www.word-of-hope.net**

To find out more

Jesus-Islam.org
A website for Christian-Muslim discussion and apologetics